DO YOU WANT A PET POTBELLIED PIG?

THAT'S AN ODD PET!

BY LOUIS MALLORY

Enslow PUBLISHING

Please visit our website, www.enslow.com. For a free color catalog of all our high-quality books, call toll free 1-800-398-2504 or fax 1-877-980-4454.

Cataloging-in-Publication Data

Names: Mallory, Louis.
Title: Do you want a pet potbellied pig? / Louis Mallory.
Description: Buffalo, NY : Enslow Publishing, 2025. | Series: That's an odd pet! | Includes glossary and index.
Identifiers: ISBN 9781978540835 (pbk.) | ISBN 9781978540842 (library bound) | ISBN 9781978540859 (ebook)
Subjects: LCSH: Potbellied pigs as pets–Juvenile literature.
Classification: LCC SF393.P74 M35 2025 | DDC 636.4'85–dc23

Published in 2025 by
Enslow Publishing
2544 Clinton Street
Buffalo, NY 14224

Portions of this work were originally authored by Pamela Tasker and published as *Potbellied Pigs*. All new material in this edition is authored by Louis Mallory.

Designer: Claire Zimmermann
Editor: Natalie Humphrey

Photo credits: Cover (photo) Irina Kozorog/Shutterstock.com; Series Art (title and heading font, texture) Gleb Guralnyk/Shutterstock.com; Series Art (background retro swirl) ChekmanDaria/Shutterstock.com; Series Art (corner dots) Romanova Ekaterina/Shutterstock.com; Series Art (body text boxes, page number background shape) Angie Makes/Shutterstock.com; Series Art (hand-drawn doodles) yugoro/Shutterstock.com; p. 5 Hakase_420/Shutterstock.com; p. 7 krolya25/Shutterstock.com; p. 9 Andrii Romanov/Shutterstock.com; p. 11 iamofoto/Shutterstock.com; p. 13 ArtSvetlana/Shutterstock.com; p. 15 cowboy54/Shutterstock.com; p. 17 MintImages/Shutterstock.com; p. 19 New Africa/Shutterstock.com.

Printed in the United States of America

CPSIA compliance information: Batch #CSENS25: For further information contact Enslow Publishing at 1-800-398-2504.

CONTENTS

Words in the glossary appear in **bold** type the first time they are used in the text.

ODD PIGS

Have you ever wondered what it would be like to live with a pig? While a farm pig might be too big for the average home, some people think a potbellied pig is the perfect pet! Potbellied pigs are much smaller than the average farm pig.

JUST THE FACTS!

In Delaware, potbellied pigs can't be kept as pets. Other states and cities will let you keep a potbellied pig, but it must stay outside in a special **enclosure**.

Make sure to check your local laws for owning a potbellied pig before getting one.

Potbellied pigs are smart, and with the right training, can even learn to do tricks. But before you pick up your potbellied pig, make sure you know what goes into raising one!

HEAVY PIGS

Potbellied pigs can be pretty heavy. Many potbellied pigs grow to be around 70 to 150 pounds (32 to 68 kg). However, some may weigh as much as 200 pounds (91 kg)!

JUST THE FACTS!

Potbellied pigs can be all black, or white with black spots. They can also be pink or white.

Potbellied pigs keep growing for around three to four years before they are fully grown.

Potbellied pigs are solid, meaning they're heavy, but their bodies are small. Most potbellied pigs are around 2 feet (0.6 m) tall. Like all pigs, potbellied pigs have hooves on their feet. Some potbellied pigs may need their hooves cut so they don't grow too long.

THE VIETNAMESE POTBELLIED PIG

Potbellied pigs might be popular in the United States, but they weren't sold in the U.S. until the mid-1980s. Potbellied pigs were originally kept as pets in Vietnam. They're a type of **miniature** pig. Potbellied pigs might not seem small, but they're much smaller than farm pigs. Farm pigs can weigh more than 1,000 pounds (453.6 kg)!

Potbellied pigs used to be raised like farm animals. But most potbellied pigs today are **bred** as pets.

The first potbellied pigs were much bigger than popular potbellied pigs today.

JUST THE FACTS!

There are at least 14 other kinds of mini pigs.

GETTING YOUR PIG

Potbellied pigs can be fun pets, but they're a lot of work! Potbellied pigs need a lot of time and money. They also need space where they can safely sleep, eat, and play.

JUST THE FACTS!

If you find you can't take care of your potbellied pig, make sure to take it to an **animal shelter** or rescue.

Some breeders may show possible pig ownerss a baby pig and pretend it's a fully grown adult.

You may find potbellied pigs at your local animal shelter. There are also people who breed potbellied pigs to sell. Make sure to ask questions to be sure the potbellied pig breeder is trustworthy. If a breeder tells you their pigs will "stay small forever," don't believe them!

A PIG HOUSE

In some places, potbellied pigs don't need to live outside. You can give your pig a safe place to live indoors. Make sure you have enough space. They need about 50 square feet (4.6 sq m). Give your pet some old newspapers or brown paper to sleep on.

JUST THE FACTS!

If you want your potbellied pig to be a house pig, make sure to pig proof your house. Potbellied pigs are curious and will chew on anything they can get their mouth on!

Just like people, potbellied pigs can get sunburns and may need special sunscreen or an enclosure to escape the sun.

If you prefer to keep your potbellied pig outside, make sure it has a windproof and rainproof house to live in. This is so it can stay warm and dry outside.

PIG FOOD

Pigs are known to eat a lot, but potbellied pigs can eat too much! To keep your pig healthy, talk to your vet about the right way to feed your pig. Younger pigs and active pigs might need more food than other pigs.

JUST THE FACTS!

You can give your potbellied pig fruits or vegetables as treats. Foods like apples, dried fruits, or nuts make great treats for potbellied pigs.

Always make sure your pig has enough fresh water to drink.

You can find potbellied pig food online or at some pet stores. You can mix this food with vegetables like broccoli and green beans. This can help make sure your pig is getting enough **nutrients** to stay healthy.

CLEAN PIGS

When you think of pigs, you might imagine a big hog rolling around in the mud. But potbellied pigs are clean animals. They don't need regular bathing. If your pig does get dirty, it's fine to hose it off. However potbellied pigs have naturally dry skin and bathing them too often can make it worse.

Potbellied pigs have **coarse** hair on their body that they shed, or lose, once or twice a year. This will make your pet itchy.

Feeding your potbellied pig healthy foods can also help keep its skin healthy.

JUST THE FACTS!

Regularly brush your potbellied pig to help it get rid of any dead skin and loose hair.

PIG VETS

Just like most pets, your potbellied pig needs trips to the vet! Before you bring your pig home, make sure a vet in your area knows how to take care of potbellied pigs. Many vets don't deal with pigs often, if ever. Potbellied pigs are not treated the same as farm animals.

JUST THE FACTS!

Just like humans, potbellied pigs can get **cavities**. Feeding your pig a healthy **diet** can help stop cavities, but some potbellied pig owners will also brush their pig's teeth!

If your pig doesn't want to eat or is acting differently than it usually does, bring it to the vet.

Take your pig to the vet for a checkup every year. Your pet needs special shots so it doesn't get **parasites** or get sick.

PIGGY FRIENDS

Potbellied pigs can make great friends! With the right care, potbellied pigs can live for 12 to 18 years. These little pigs are so smart, they can be trained to do more than tricks. Those that live inside can be trained to use the bathroom outside!

Potbellied pigs love to play with toys and enjoy time lying in a shady place. Some potbellied pigs will also enjoy taking walks outside!

TAKING CARE OF YOUR POTBELLIED PIG!

Give your potbellied pig a safe place to sleep on newspapers or brown paper.

Make sure your potbellied pig stays out of direct sunlight to prevent sunburns.

Give your pig fresh drinking water.

Feed your potbellied pig food meant for it and never overfeed them.

You can give your potbellied pig treats, but be sure to limit them.

Make sure a vet in your area can care for your pig before you bring your pig home.

JUST THE FACTS!

If you want to take your pig for a walk, you can buy it a **harness**. Remember that your pig might be heavy, strong, and **stubborn**, so you may want to bring an adult on your walk with you.

GLOSSARY

animal shelter: A place where people take lost animals or animals without an owner.

breed: To mate two animals with desired qualities in order to produce more like them. Breeders are people who breed certain animals, such as cattle, pigs, and dogs.

cavity: An empty space or hole in a tooth that can grow over time.

coarse: Thick and rough.

diet: The food an animal usually eats.

enclosure: An area surrounded by a fence to stop an animal from getting out.

harness: Straps around an animal that allow someone to control it.

miniature: Something that is small for its kind.

nutrients: Something a living thing needs to grow and stay alive.

parasite: A living thing that lives on, in, or with another living thing and often harms it.

stubborn: Unwilling to change one's mind.

FOR MORE INFORMATION

Books

Rodriguez, Alicia. *Potbellied Pig.* Coral Springs, FL: Seahorse Publishing, 2022.

Siemens, Jared. *Potbellied Pig.* New York, NY: AV2, 2024.

Websites

National Geographic Kids: Hamming It Up
www.kids.nationalgeographic.com/pages/article/hamming-it-up
Learn about some amazing tricks and watch videos of Nellie, the pet potbellied pig!

Wild Animal Safari: 10 Pot Bellied Pig Facts
www.animalsafari.com/10-pot-belly-pig-facts/
Find out more about potbellied pigs.

INDEX